Tethered

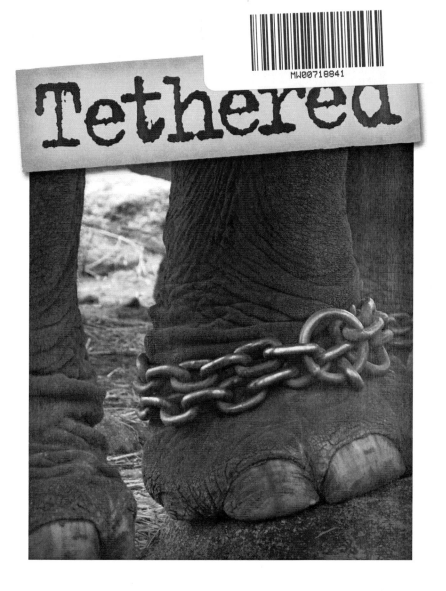

Breaking the Chains
of the Shackled Church

Dr. Tim E. Miller

IMD Press

Westminster, Colorado

Tethered: Breaking the Chains of the Shackled Church

ISBN 13: 978-0-9817335-8-6
Printed in the United States of America

Published by IMD Press
7140 Hooker Street
Westminster, CO 80030
www.imdpress.com

Contents

Part 1: The Tethered Church

Part 2: The Untethered Church

Acknowledgements

The sum of what a man becomes is the result of a compilation of influences upon his life. Some of these influences are circumstantial and others are by choice, but all are divinely orchestrated. My parents and family have had a major impact upon my life and have largely shaped my pilgrimage of faith. My closest friends have left a stamp of spiritual camaraderie that has encouraged my walk with Jesus. How wonderful it has been to roam together throughout this vast expanse called life. The body of Christ, who has exhibited much patience with me as I have hopped from one theological marker to the next, has aided the discovery of all contained herein. The thoughts and words of Herb Hodges, my mentor and friend, are scattered throughout this work, although I cannot cite him for most of my conclusions.

Thanks to the men who "accidentally" saw the Tethered icon on my laptop and requested an unedited copy. Your encouragement to finish this task has made all the difference in motivation. Otherwise, this small project would still be shelved.

Thanks to Dan Wilmoth for wrestling with me through the issues of this book and for taking the picture for the cover. You are not only my traveling partner but one of my dearest friends.

Pain has been my lingering friend throughout the many months of the past after the death of my precious wife, Lane Ann, to colon cancer. She is the one who *really* paid the price for this book as she endured many years of deep soul searching that produced this work.

Thanks to Cecilia for your additional input and help in the editing process. Your influence upon my life has already cast a bright ray of hope for the future.

Preface

I have approached this brief work with brokenness and repentance. Most of what is contained in this book was revealed to me by God's Spirit during deep times of reflection and questioning. For many years I have wrestled with the issues contained herein. The questions have been ever so apparent, but the answers have been quite elusive. I suppose someone must live long enough to experience a variety of life's challenges before he can freely and cautiously attempt to answer the great complexities of life. Many of them are never quite realized. However, despite the many years of wrestling with the issues contained herein, I didn't know how to articulate my conclusions. Now that I am forty-eight years of age and have pastored six churches, I now have something to say. Most of the issues discussed in this book stab my heart due to my personal mistakes as a leader. Much of what is addressed is controversial and problematic in terms of that which hinders the church's biblical directive. I do not have an axe to grind, but a Sword to sharpen. My observations are not intended to be critical but explanatory. Additionally, this small work is not intended to be a theological treatise of the subjects brought forward but a simple introduction to the issues at hand. It is hoped the interested reader will conduct a more extensive research of his own.

Furthermore, the opinions relating to the topics addressed in the following pages are unapologetically subjective and open for debate. I'm not sure I would want to read a book and not clearly understand the author's stance on the subjects addressed. For some, the opinions depicted in this book may seem heretical. However, I do not shrink back for calling God's leaders in focus with His Word. Indeed, over the course of time, The Way has become cloudy. The murky vision of the church has generated many trails of style and leadership with multiple strategies in tow. And for many years, I have wondered *why*.

While attending a Promise Keepers Conference during the mid 1990s, I noticed many of the men in our group experiencing profound movements of God upon their lives. The thought occurred to me, "If these men respond like they normally do, within a few weeks, they will be back to normal." The tragedy of that thought buried my face into my hands as I sat interceding for my brothers. Then, I asked the Lord a question. "Why, Oh Lord, do they lose their enthusiasm for you so quickly?" Two hours later, the Lord spoke to me very clearly and this is what He said, "Because they are prisoners of *The System* too." That last little word is what bothered me most—the word *too*.

The Lord Jesus had referred to the church as the "system of men." And not only that, but I was imprisoned by it also. Upon deeper reflection, I realized I was tethered by the system and to the system. That word from the Lord explained much of my spiritual struggle for many years as a leader. And it has everything to do with why I am writing this book.

I am concerned as eastern religions invade our western culture our weak form of institutional Christianity will become lost among the many other manuals of religious orthodoxy. The world needs to see a vibrant empowered church of biblical proportions. May leaders across our land hear the voice of the Lord calling, "Let my people go." May Christian leaders have the spiritual fortitude to raise the banner of biblical adherence so that future generations can clearly walk the path of obedience. We dare not fail to hear His voice in these last days. It is my hope and passion for a new generation of leaders to grab the reins of leadership in reckless abandonment to His beckoning call. Only then, will the people of God march with His standard of power and become overwhelmed with His consuming mandate to make disciples.

The church is a boot camp and we are at war. May the flimsy, pretentious form we now embrace be cast off for the garment of praise and surrender. May self-promotion, self-sufficiency, and self-preservation be drowned out by the roar of God's people entering the battle arena. We have a mission to fulfill. We must hear His voice calling, "This is the way, walk in it!" It is my prayer this small work will ignite the hearts and minds of God's leaders who will lead the church to fulfill Christ's commission until He returns.

Introduction

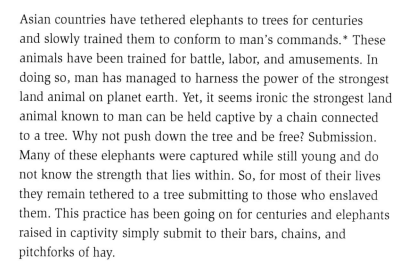

Tethered

Asian countries have tethered elephants to trees for centuries
and slowly trained them to conform to man's commands.* These
animals have been trained for battle, labor, and amusements. In
doing so, man has managed to harness the power of the strongest
land animal on planet earth. Yet, it seems ironic the strongest land
animal known to man can be held captive by a chain connected
to a tree. Why not push down the tree and be free? Submission.
Many of these elephants were captured while still young and do
not know the strength that lies within. So, for most of their lives
they remain tethered to a tree submitting to those who enslaved
them. This practice has been going on for centuries and elephants
raised in captivity simply submit to their bars, chains, and
pitchforks of hay.

Today, there is a more perplexing irony occurring in the Christian
church than that of the mighty elephant. When the Holy Spirit
came at Pentecost, He came with the greatest power ever known
to man. He came with explosive power to equip the church to
uproot anything in her way. He gave her the ability to leave tracks
throughout the jungles of time that no one could refute belonged
to God's people. He genetically infused the church with Himself
so that her offspring would exhibit the greatest power on earth—

the power to heal, transform, redeem, and set others free from the chains that bind them. Yet, this church is all but free and neither is she empowered to break the chains of evil. Consequently, we have not left an imprint of God's glory for others to see. Without realizing the great power within to break the chains that bind us, we remain tethered—submitted to the battles directed by men, labors demanded by the organization, and politics dictated by the denominational circus. And while we roam around behind our self-made bars, the world mocks our lack of power and throws us peanuts.

There is a great army of believers longing to be free from the hindrances of today's institutional entanglements. They are honestly aware of their lack of freedom both inwardly and outwardly. Admittedly, instead of being inextricably bound to the cross, they are tethered to stubborn hardwoods whose ecclesiastical roots have intermingled for centuries. These believers long to fulfill their God-given calling and hear their Master say, "well done." Even so, the real work of ministry is still not taking place. Real work referring to equipping the saints to multiply their lives (Matthew 28:18-20). This is God's only plan for reaching the world—disciple making. This small book was written to unveil why the work of discipleship is not taking place as well as to expose the well rooted forces that hold so many captive. It is also our hope to provide a biblical way of escape. May our hearts dance in ecstatic discovery as our new found freedom leaves a path well traveled for future generations to follow.

*Quotes referring to the training of wild elephants were taken from internet article *Elephant care manual for Mahouts* (pronounced may-hoots) *and camp manager*, www.fao.org.

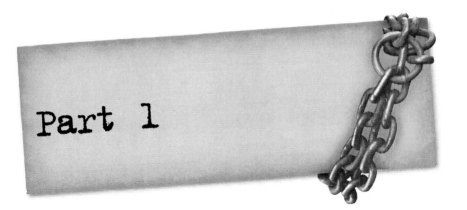

Part 1

The Tethered Church

Chapter One

Tethered to Institutionalism

*A chained elephant with plenty of food and water
is far less likely to try to break its chains than a
hungry or thirsty elephant with little food or water
inside its chaining area.*

Institutionalism has provided a safe harbor for God's children to
rest. Instead of equipping the saints for ministry to the world, we
have provided a sanctuary where the basic felt needs of the people
can be met. This gentle atmosphere doesn't require much of the
people and many elect to join the system. They enter into the ranks
of the institutional church with all the perks of membership.

In the same way elephants were meant to be wild and free
roaming, God's children were meant to radically enter the arena
of the world with explosive impact. Sadly, many leaders have
accepted their chains and no longer lead the people of God
in their quest for freedom. As a result, the church has been
domesticated. We no longer ferociously hate sin and earnestly
contend for the faith. For generations we have been comfortably
tethered and thus forgotten our original design. We remain
politely behind our man-made reserves trumpeting for our needs

to be met, all the while grazing in the fields of indifference to the real things of God.

Clearly, this is not how the New Testament church was originally ordained to function. This predicament of the modern church demands that we in the very least explore three areas of concern:

- God's plan for His people to become a living organism.
- The gradual corruption of God's design for church leadership.
- The detrimental consequences of forsaking God's plan for leading, growing, and maturing people.

One of the culprits preventing the church from becoming a living organism is institutionalism. Institutionalism occurs when God's people become almost completely focused upon *preserving* the livelihood of the organization; Whereas, the better biblical paradigm of the church existing as an organism, is consecrated to *producing* life in others. Institutionalism focuses upon self-preservation in hopes of sustaining the organization, while the church as a living organism focuses upon self-sacrifice for the expansion of God's Kingdom. Organisms naturally reproduce in like kind. Organizations do not.

It appears in the early days of the church, the people of "the Way" were a living organism who greatly impacted the culture of their day, especially the religious establishment (Acts 9:2).

They were not an organization although they were organized. God had given them the power to turn their world upside down and through persecution, scattered them like seeds throughout the Roman Empire and the rest of the world. The good news of Jesus spread rapidly as those believing in Him met in one another's homes and worshiped, prayed and shared together.

Initially God appointed gifted leaders for mobilizing the saints both for maturity and ministry (Ephesians 4:11-13). These gifts to the church came in the form of people endowed spiritually by God and included apostles, prophets, evangelists, pastors, and teachers. Let us examine briefly the biblical description and purpose for each designation of leadership. The following descriptions are based upon the functionality of each office as they are performed in the biblical story line.

The Apostle

The apostle was to be the catalyst through which the world-wide missionary imperative of the church was carried out. He kept the church's vision focused outward. The apostle was uniquely and specifically called to international work and shared in the process of church planting, evangelism and discipleship. According to examples in the Bible, the apostle was to be the visionary leader who held the churches together and acted as an objective go-between during disputes by utilizing Scriptures as the directive for discerning right from wrong during the resolution of conflicts. As every believer, the apostle also acted as an apologist or defender of Christian doctrine. He was not the head of the church for Jesus was (and is) the absolute authority in all matters of polity.[1]

Some point to Paul's defense of his apostleship to emphasize their conviction apostles no longer exist due to the fact they could not have actually seen Jesus or raised anyone from the dead (1 Corinthians 9:1). However, Paul was not saying since he had seen Jesus then all apostles must do so in order to be recognized as an apostle. He was simply using this fact to clarify his calling to these first century skeptics. Furthermore, many others saw Christ and they were not recognized as apostles, including over five hundred who saw Jesus after his resurrection and were not uniquely declared apostles either. To say there are no longer apostles because Jesus can no longer be seen is stretching what Paul was saying.

Additionally, to say apostles do not exist because people are no longer being raised from the dead (Acts 9:39-40) is to make an uneducated statement. There are documented cases around the world of this phenomenon occasionally taking place. By "documented" I am referring to the testimonies of eye witnesses which are used frequently in the Bible itself to prove truthful accounts. Even our modern courts take eye witnesses very seriously when determining guilt or innocence. Furthermore, if the purpose for this specific kind of miracle was to give God glory (John 11:4), then why wouldn't the Lord still perform such a miracle? I would wholeheartedly agree that personal experience alone is not a valid test for truth and just because something supernaturally occurs does not necessarily mean it is from God. However, I am disappointed when believers deny and reject these supernatural miracles without investigation. Mostly, this is due to their inexperience and because such things do not fit into their doctrinal box. Each supernatural occurrence must be examined in light of the biblical evidence. God can do what He wants to do when He wants to do it.

Apostles are still used by God to perform miracles, but "seeing Jesus" is not a prerequisite for this office. Even if modern apostles did see Jesus—if they saw Him in the same manner as Paul—they would not be received by many who claim this criteria for apostleship for these same people no longer believe in "visions" either. Consequently, the gift of apostleship has been altogether ignored in most churches, especially non-charismatic protestant assemblies.

Furthermore, while I would reject the formalistic and powerless claim of the Catholic Church to appoint apostolic leaders today, I equally reject the claim from most Protestant churches that genuine apostles ceased to exist after the first century. Why? Because it doesn't make sense for God to give gifts to the Church for "the equipping of the saints for the work of service"

(Ephesians 4:11-13) and then remove them after the first century—especially since we know God's will to be for all of His children to reach spiritual maturity. Accordingly, this is one of the primary reasons He gave apostles to the church. Secondly, not everyone was equipped or had reached maturity after the death of the original apostles. Did God simply nullify the future need for apostolic ministry after He appointed the original twelve? If so, there shouldn't be biblical references to apostles other than the twelve—but there are (Romans 16:7, Acts 2:37; 14:4; 15: 4,22, 1 Corinthians 12:28, 2 Corinthians chapters 1–7, 11:13, Ephesians 3:5; 4:11, 2 Peter 3:2, Revelation 2:2; 18:20).

The Prophet

The prophet was a combination of a New Covenant proclaimer (forthteller) and an Old Testament foreteller. The prophet's message was hard and forthright and often very stark and abrasive in its description. The function of the prophetic message was to keep the people of God from calcifying in self-righteousness—to keep the hearts of God's people soft and pliable, always ready to receive and obey His Word. The prophet's message kept the church pure and discouraged gradual compromise which inevitably led to the weakening consequences of internal sin. There were occasions when the prophet would warn the church of future events.[2] In most churches today, the fiery voice of the prophet has been extinguished by four-point outlines and sermonic rhetoric.

The Evangelist

The work of the evangelist was to carry the evangelistic thrust of the church. This person was uniquely gifted to share in the equipping of the saints. The evangelist led the charge both in example and practice as the people of God shared their faith within their families and communities. Like the prophet, the evangelist was given the responsibility to preach God's truths (2 Timothy 4:2-5, Acts 21:8). In many churches the evangelist has been turned into a professional circuit rider preaching to churches instead of a lost world.

The Pastor

Some would classify the last two gifts mentioned in Ephesians 4:11 as one—pastor/teacher. Even so, we will deal with them as two separate gifts. The pastor was called by God to shepherd the flock—albeit, his first responsibility was to equip the saints for ministry both toward one another and to the world (Ephesians 4:12). The pastor was to nurture God's children by feeding, caring, protecting, and loving them. He taught them how to love God, one another, and their fellow man [1 Timothy 3:1-7, Titus 1:7-11 (as an overseer), 1 Peter 5:2 (as an elder)]. In many churches today, the "pastoral gift" listed in Ephesians chapter four, is the only one functioning.

The Teacher

The teacher was responsible for instructing God's people in the ways of righteousness through biblical exhortation and example. He was to train and equip other believers to become self-feeding disciples of Jesus who reproduced in like kind (Acts 13:1, 1 Corinthians 12:28, 2 Timothy 2:2, Hebrews 5:12, James 3:1, 2 Peter 2:1). Most Christian teaching today is centered on personal spiritual growth instead of equipping the saints for maturity *and* multiplication.

Elders and Deacons

Additionally, we must also consider the biblical role of elders and deacons. The terms elder, bishop, and overseer are used interchangeably throughout the New Testament. The only text that uses the actual term "pastor" is Ephesians 4:11. Therefore, it is reasonable to assume the pastor was intended to be an elder himself and quite feasibly would assume the role as the leader of elders. The qualifications for an overseer are almost identical for the qualifications listed for elders (see related texts under paragraph describing "The Pastor" on previous page as well as 1 Timothy 5:17). Thus, it seems the New Testament depicts a plurality of leaders for the body of Christ. These leaders are gifted by God and affirmed through the body of Christ. But how do these leaders receive their offices of ministry? It appears the elders were appointed (not elected by popular consensus) by the apostles and other church leaders such as Titus.

Titus is only mentioned by name in 2 Corinthians, Galatians, 2 Timothy, and Titus. Yet, it is very strongly evidenced that Titus was with Paul throughout much of his missionary ministry which apparently gave him a reasonable degree of credibility as a leader (recorded in Acts 2, 2 Corinthians 8:23). Titus was also a pastor in Crete. One thing is certain, Titus was ordered by Paul to "appoint elders in every city" (Titus 12:5).

In Acts 14:23, Paul and Barnabas appoint elders in Derbe, Lystra, Iconium, and Antioch. In many of these cases, there is no indication of vast amounts of time passing before the elders were appointed and there certainly was not an educational requirement beyond normal discipleship. It seems the Holy Spirit had much to do with this appointing process throughout the apostolic ministry.

Deacons were chosen by the body of believers to act as servants (Acts 6:3). Consequently, they were never given decision-making power for the church. Secondly, they were to be "filled with the Spirit" of God and they were to be "tested" and proven *before* they were even allowed to wait on tables (1 Timothy 3:10). Interestingly enough, they were often depicted as performing "signs and wonders" (Acts 6:8).

It is very clear God had placed leaders in position to propagate a very well-balanced empowered organism that would flourish throughout the Church Age. Although the church would never be perfect, the proper leaders were in place to provide a system of checks and balances to ensure the purpose of God's people would never be thwarted prior to the second coming of Christ. In review, the New Testament church had God-appointed leaders (apostles, prophets, evangelists, pastors, and teachers)—and these appointed leaders further appointed leaders (elders, overseers, and pastors) and servants chosen by the body of Christ (i.e. deacons).

Institutionalized Church

Satan's strategy to disease the living organism of the church ensued very quickly after the first century—*never* allow God's people to mature to the point of multiplication. He effectively implanted this strategy by diminishing the importance of the leaders listed in Ephesians chapter four. Remember, God had very specifically given the five-fold ministry leaders for this purpose—to mature His followers. If the church embraced God's plan for maturation, then Satan was bent upon at the very least—corrupting the leaders themselves. Secondly, if he could not corrupt these leaders, then maybe he could convince the church to partially embrace God's plan. This way, both the leaders and the church would forever be confused when it came to the functionality and purpose of leadership. As a result, the leaders of the church who were accepted would inevitably become so weighted down with ministry responsibilities that healthy multiplication would be impossible.

Around 313 A.D. the emperor Constantine declared Christianity to be the official religion of the Roman Empire. This announcement had cataclysmic consequences to the early church—an event which has tethered us to institutionalism to this very day. Slowly the structure of the church began to change in the areas of leadership and polity. A sharp distinction was made between clergy and laity and essentially two classes of believers were established—those who could hear God and those who could not. The clergy assumed the role of dictating to everyone else what God was saying. As the people gradually submitted, the church began to digress from a living organism ruled by God and led by His Spirit into an organization ruled by leaders appointed by men. Unfortunately, over time, many traditions of men and organizational structures became unquestionably accepted as biblically authoritative. Much later, the Protestant Reformation corrected many doctrinal, traditional, and biblical heresies, but seemingly did little to reform the role of church leaders established during this same era. Consequently, the function of these leaders has remained virtually the same for centuries, causing the church to almost completely institutionalize herself.

Tragically, the modern church has learned to operate without most of these very important leaders mentioned in Ephesians chapter four. In fact, we have been operating so long without them, it almost seems heretical when someone mentions our apostasy. Consequently, when the New Testament model is upheld, leaders today no longer recognize its authenticity. Institutionalism has gradually corrupted, weakened, and replaced God's appointed leadership.

Now, let us examine the consequences of forsaking God's original plan in exchange for the institutionalism of our day. Church leaders are increasingly confused concerning their respective calling, appointment, and function in the modern church. Because God's appointed leaders are mysteriously missing, there is great debate over what constitutes a calling from God and how one should respond to it. If someone today senses a "call" into full-time Christian service, the first thing the institutional church usually does is suggest the need to further their education by attending seminary.

Secondly, they must decide which field of ministry into which they are called. Within the recent past, the church has added many tracks for full-time ministry candidates—pastor, associate pastor, music, education, youth, children, evangelism, or missions (this doesn't take into consideration the many offshoots from these tracks that have been added in the last few decades). Only two of these are directly mentioned in Ephesians 4:11 (pastor, evangelist). The church has created a categorical chasm between the full-time professionals and the part-time ill-equipped.

In retrospect, if the church were doing a good job of equipping the saints for ministry, there would be no further need for education. The biblical example of teaching, mentoring, and turning loose should be sufficient to train new leaders. However, this is usually not the case today and therefore those called into ministry have few choices if they want to earn a living while doing ministry. In essence, they are forced to fulfill the expectations of the congregation which eventually results in many leaders serving in the wrong capacity. Furthermore, every believer is called to be on mission full-time. This lack of understanding concerning the role and calling of church leaders has created much distress in the body of Christ. Many leaders today are not serving within their gifted arena. To complicate matters, the institutional system in which they are trying to serve doesn't provide an appropriate channel to carry out their God appointed calling.

Institutionalized Leadership

Consider the following examples. [When the term "pastor" is in quotations, it refers to the church's traditional expectation of the pastor's role. When pastor is used without quotations, the interpretation is that of Ephesians 4 previously explored.]

If someone is genuinely appointed by God to be a prophet and becomes a "pastor," his messages will be extremely confrontational. The prophet's heart is for authentic revival, confession, and repentance. He longs for the people of God to develop a deep passion for Christ and his messages reflect this. He clearly sees the institutional abuses within the church and seeks to expose every biblical inconsistency. His passion alone eventually gives reason for those to oppose him. Accordingly, the prophet's message is a threat to the comfort zone of the institutional establishment. Because of his passion and deep convictions, the prophet is usually well received in the beginning, but after awhile, the congregation gets tired of fiery messages on repentance and holiness. They secretly desire another orator. And rightly so, the prophet is not called to proclaim judgment every Sunday. His proclamation should be occasional when God's people drift into sin. He knows his messages are weighty and longs for something more conceivably "lovable or soft" to say, but the Lord will not give him such. Why? Because he is a prophet. The prophet's messages keep the church from becoming calcified in self-righteousness. He is called by God to occasionally say, "Thus saith the Lord."

Prophets were not tolerated very well in the Old Testament and neither are they in today's church. Most prophets do not last long as "pastors" and congregations usually misunderstand their passion for anger, coupled with the fact most of the prophet's energy is spent on preaching instead of pastoral duties. It is my belief most prophets do not enjoy pastoral ministry and deep within their inner recesses wonder *why*—never understanding they were called to be a prophet instead of a "pastor."

So the prophet leaves the local church (or is forcefully terminated) and the congregation begins searching for a new "pastor." From their perception the last "pastor" didn't love them although admittedly, "he was a good preacher." They suggest the committee (or denominational hierarchy) find someone who has strong pastoral gifts who will love and nurture instead of browbeat. The committee follows suit and presents someone to the congregation with strong pastoral gifts. The new "pastor" does the expected job well and people love him for awhile— perhaps a very long while since this type giftedness lends itself to longevity. However, if the "pastor" is not exceptionally gifted in the pulpit, people eventually begin to make statements like, "Our leader is a great 'pastor' and we love him, but he sure isn't much of a preacher and we are starving spiritually." Occasionally, churches will find someone with a gift/mix for a "pastor" who is also a good public speaker. This type minister is best suited for the system as it runs today. Woe to the prophet who follows a loving "pastor" who has had longevity. If one follows the pattern long enough in most churches, it is almost comical to watch the pattern repetitiously switch back and forth from pastor to prophet.

Suppose an evangelist becomes a "pastor." Generally, the church will see an upsurge in people coming to Christ and everyone will be excited about the new people in the church—until it comes time to share leadership positions with those new people—or, they do not represent the same racial or socio-economic level of the older established membership. Problems quickly ensue. The people complain they are weary of hearing salvation messages and begrudge the fact they are not getting fed. Due to the sociological upheaval, self-centeredness, and changes that are orchestrated by numerical growth, the evangelist serving as "pastor" eventually finds himself looking for a new place of ministry. Those led to the Lord Jesus during his ministry are often embittered and isolated because he is no longer their mentor and trusted leader. They are confused as to why he left them.

I knew a man called to be an evangelist who was serving as a "pastor." He declared, "The only reason I pastor this church is so I can lead people to Jesus." He went on to describe his distaste for the pastoral ministry. I tried to explain to him *why* he felt that way, but he had no frame of reference from which to understand my comments. The evangelist serving as "pastor" finds himself very discouraged with pastoral ministry. After all, doesn't the church want others coming to Christ? From his perspective, this is the most important function of the church. Rightly so, God created and called him to be this way.

Many times churches will have teachers for "pastors" and everyone loves learning the deep things of God under his leadership. But not many get saved under his ministry neither does the church grow numerically. Eventually people begin to murmur even against the expositor. The church may indeed grow from the transfer of believers from other churches, but these people are usually fleeing their "pastor," the evangelist!

The teacher serving as "pastor" is usually described by the congregation as a hermit because he spends most of his time studying while locking himself into the church office. The congregation becomes dissatisfied since much of the pastoral ministry is neglected. All the while, the teacher believes his expository teaching makes up for this weakness. God wired him to be a teacher, not a "pastor." Great teachers must spend great amounts of time in study.

How much discipleship training will occur in situations such as these? The results will be almost nil. Most congregations freely accept more than one teacher in the body of Christ (other than the pastor) although in most incidences teachers either sign up or are elected in response to their recommendation from a committee or because they are teachers by profession. Many times these teachers serve out of obligation since there is no one else who will do it. Soon their time has been served and the entire annual process starts over again, although they sometimes manage to maintain a good attitude about it all.

So if we can embrace the concept of more than one teacher in a given congregation, then why haven't we embraced the possibility of more than one pastor, prophet, or evangelist within the same congregation? They are present. In the absence of God's appointed leaders (five-fold ministry), many churches have ignored the other appointed leaders called elders. Consequently, they have no other leaders except paid staff and deacons. To fill this vacancy, deacons have become the major administrative leaders in many churches. To add insult to injury, most of these leaders have never been tested and many of them are not "full of the Spirit." Yet, many pastors and churches are led by the popular consensus or recommendations of the deacon body. Conflict, power control, and short-term pastorates are the result. Very little long-term ministry occurs while churches haggle and split over the most minute things. Is there anyone out there asking *why*? We have completely ignored the simple explanations and directives of Scripture when it comes to leadership and accountability.

Although the belief system of many in doctrine and practice may not accept God's original design for "maturing the saints," God's Holy Spirit is *still* calling men and women to fulfill the roles He originally intended for them as described in Ephesians 4:11. Ministry in the modern church can be very confusing, unfruitful, and unfulfilling for those appointed to fulfill the leadership offices originally appointed by God. The reason being, the body of Christ no longer provides a place for these individuals to serve. As a result, among these leaders there is restlessness within and a complete dissatisfaction with the institutional system we call the church. Deep within these leaders know that something is amiss. (Those *truly* called to serve as pastors do not sense this as much).

> *Whenever the elephant must transport the chain between two places, usually the night time tethering site and the work site, never make it drag the chain when it is attached to the foot. The massive weight can cause the elephant to sprain or dislocate its ankle.*

There remains no effective vehicle of change through which to impact the existing institutional church. Consequently, many leaders are getting tired of dragging the chain of institutional expectations and dropping out of the ministry altogether. This massive emotional weight is doing irreparable damage to leaders and their families. Many are internally wounded and suffer from acute burn out. As a result, the joy of ministry has long since dissipated.

These simple examples depict how Institutionalism has clouded the understanding of many churches as well as its leaders when it comes to Ephesians 4:11-13. In the meantime, we run the institutional course—missing God's best, all the while tethered to the traditions of men.

[1] Philippians 1:16, Acts chapters 13–28, Romans 16:7, 1 Corinthians chapters 1–14, 1 Timothy chapters 1–6, 2 Corinthians chapters 10–13, Galatians chapters 1–2, Hebrews, 2 Peter, 2 John, 3 John, Jude, Acts 26.

[2] Joel 2:12-17, Amos chapters 3–6, Malachi 1:6–3:18, Matthew 10:41, Acts 13:6, 21:10, 1 Corinthians 14:27, 1 Timothy 1:12, Exodus 15:20, Judges 4:4, Luke 2:36, Acts 21:8-9.

Chapter Two

Tethered to Traditionalism

*Tethering chains are fixed to one front foot
(usually the right) with the other end secured
to an anchoring point, usually a tree.*

Why the right leg? Why not chain the left leg? In all probability,
this is the way it's always been done. Or, to put it another way,
it's tradition.

I would like to define traditionalism as establishing the church's
leadership roles, polity and authority according to the traditional
expectations of men as opposed to the directives of Scripture.
In other words, we have learned to conduct the matters of the
church according to the expectations of people without input
from the Most High God. The following descriptions show how
traditional expectations typically affect the local church and
answer the three most basic questions: Who leads us? Who
makes the decisions? Who carries the authority? My personal
question to you is this, "Does the typical church answer these
three questions in light of God's biblical design or according to
the design of men?"

Leadership: Who Leads Us?

Churches today will fight both tooth and nail if one starts
changing their leadership structure (who is responsible for what).
Pastors and other church staff have a much unspoken (sometimes
outspoken) job description. If they do not fulfill expectations from
the congregation, then rebuke usually follows. This rebuke either
comes from the deacons, committees, or denominational heads
(depending upon the denomination). Interestingly enough, rarely
do any of these self-appointed vigilantes fall into the category of
God's appointed leaders. They are virtually all elected by men.
There are many church staff leaders today who are not happy nor
fulfilled as they tiptoe around the traditional expectations of their
ministries to perform. They say, "That's just the way it is." I have
heard this statement by church staff members more times than
I can count. As one pastor shared his heart with me, he stated,
"Every morning as I unlock my office, I ask myself the question,
'Is this really what I am called to do?'"

How can church leaders fulfill their God appointed roles when they
spend most of their time oiling the machinery of organizational
expectations? The first calling of the pastor is to equip the saints
for ministry (Ephesians 4:12). As a result, the saints should
be doing the ministry. Yet, many pastors spend very little time
training and equipping others because their job descriptions are
filled with traditional expectations for maintaining the institution.
For instance, the pastor who misses a wedding, funeral, hospital
visit, birth, or business meeting will find himself in great trouble
indeed. Additionally, administrating the church and counseling
take considerable time and effort. None of these responsibilities
mentioned in the previous two sentences is listed specifically
in Scripture as the pastor's primary responsibility. Yet, they are
consuming almost every pastor in today's traditional church. In
essence, under traditionalism, the church dictates to the pastor

what he should be doing. Why? Because some leaders in the past succumbed to the pressure and bowed beneath the yoke of traditionalism—consequently, every successive leader is expected to do the same. Other staff members face the same dilemma. We have drifted away from the original blueprint of God's design to the extent no one seems to notice. In fact, the average person who regularly attends church services probably could not state what the pastor is supposed to do outside the expectations just mentioned. As a result, even among church staff leaders, there is great confusion over following God amidst the constant pressure to stay in the traditional box of congregational expectations.

The absence of God-appointed leaders means diminished impact. Due to the absence of apostolic leadership, the church is missing the world-wide impact depicted in the Bible. I am not referring to missions but to something much greater. Without the prophet whose preaching purifies the church and keeps her from cementing in self-righteousness, the church is filled with worldliness and sin of every kind. Without the evangelist, who has been turned into a professional circuit rider who usually preaches to churches filled (or half-filled) with professing believers, most churches are not leading others to Christ. From God's original blueprint to reach the world by utilizing the five-fold ministry directive, the church today is attempting to accomplish this purpose using only two—pastor and teacher. Many would even classify these two gifts as one.

The average congregation is perfectly contented to allow their pastor to love, nurture, and care for them completely ignoring the out-of-balance system they have embraced. In so doing, without the presence of the other supportive and related gifts (apostles, prophets, evangelists, and teachers) the church naturally spirals into maintenance mode without worldwide impact, purity, evangelistic growth, or spiritual maturity. These are the brand marks of traditionalism.

Polity: Who Makes the Decisions?

When referring to "polity," I am referring to the practical organization of the church—services, programs, and decision-making. In many cases the organizational structure of the church is hallowed ground for those who have become satisfied with spiritual lethargy and apathy. In their opinion, nothing is wrong with the church as long as their personal comfort zone is not challenged. This predominant "me-ism" has ushered into being a very self-centered, self-reliant, faithless, prayerless, and powerless church—albeit very comfortable. The New Testament church was focused upon *explosion* while today's traditional church is programmed for *implosion*. We have organized ourselves for certain failure in fulfilling Christ's commission as we move in exactly the opposite direction He mandated. Let us examine a few more areas that have been greatly contorted by traditionalism.

Consider the typical traditional Sunday morning worship service. Remember, traditionalism leans heavily upon the past. Each week, many churches hold to the same identical format as they have been for decades. Consequently, they have a stand up—sit down ritual. The offering is received during the same time period in each service. The only thing with fluidity is the songs they sing which seem to be repeated at least bi-monthly. The sermon is preached followed by an invitation in most protestant congregations. Sunday evening follows the same type of format. Wednesday (or other midweek) evenings are a little different and form varies from congregation to congregation.

Theoretically, it is quite possible to maintain this same format for years and years without ever seeing a significant movement of God. This type ritual is somehow supposed to invoke the presence of God into our midst. How could we have drifted into such dead, repetitious form in order to seek the Lord? The puzzling thing is hundreds and thousands of people seem to think (at least, in part) going through this ritual every week is what it means to be "Christian." Traditional repetition has a way of blinding the eyes and waxing cold the heart. Can anyone who practices this predictable cycle remember what it was like to truly be in the presence of God?

What happened to Moses during his experience with the burning bush? How about Isaiah when he saw the vision of heaven? What about Solomon when the glory of God fell upon the temple? What happened to Paul on the road to Damascus? These events were hardly nonchalant or casual. God doesn't always move with such astonishing displays, but when He does move—when He is truly present—lives are forever changed—no one sleeps, and no one is bored. And although we should not live *for* these movements of God, I sure do not want to live *without* them. Unfortunately, our systematic organization has replaced God's imminent presence. Spontaneity and sensitivity to the Spirit's leadership have been eclipsed by form and time constraints. While we sleep through our time honored traditions—people are perishing without Christ. The absence of balanced leadership within the organizational structure has bred boredom and discontentedness among God's people as our time honored traditions lull us into apathetic restlessness.

Concerning polity which extends beyond the local church, various assemblies have developed substitutes (which replace the biblical model) to connect themselves with other churches. These denominations have set up hierarchal structures whereby churches supposedly stay connected and work together with churches of like kind. This connective church structure ensures the majority of proposed work will be carried out by the few. Accordingly, since individual autonomy is maintained, real biblical cohesiveness or unity is never achieved. Rarely is there a common vision carried out with corporate zeal. Instead of being one church led by One, we have become many churches led by many. Is there any wonder why we are not fulfilling The Great Commission of Christ? Each church is trying to reach the same goal, but we are trying to accomplish it through our own personal means and vision. Anyone with eyes to see would have to admit there is very little unity or common vision among the body of Christ in America. When I speak of unity, I am not referring to the absence of strife but unity of purpose. Churches remain segregated, divided, and skeptical towards one another—especially towards those outside their denomination. Although much work can be done through the sharing of financial resources and manpower, it doesn't come close to what could happen if every group of believers were on a unified mission. God's appointed leaders have been replaced by denominational structures. Consequently, denominational organizations have only widened the chasm of hope for biblical unity within the Body of Christ. Why? Because God did not appoint denominations to do the work of apostles, prophets, evangelists, pastors, and teachers—He appointed *people*. Our man made efforts to unite the body of Christ are falling drastically short of the man power needed to reach the world.

Authority: Who Carries the Authority?

Traditionalism has not only defined the church's leadership roles and polity, but her authority as well. By authority, I am referring to the governing principles of the Body. When democracy crept into the church, traditionalism played its greatest trump card. This process allows the most immature believers to have equal voting power with the most mature leaders in the body. If the immature believers outnumber the mature believers (leaders) then it is quite possible for the entire church to be led by immature decisions. Can you imagine any corporation in America making its decisions in this manner? The results would be devastating. This predicament sets the stage for the political game to begin as congregational authority replaces the plurality of spiritual leaders the Scripture ordains. Yet, if this traditional authority is questioned, it is immediately perceived as a power play for control of the church. Control is the issue here. Pastors are afraid of congregational control and congregations are afraid of pastoral control. Why are we afraid for God to be in control?

This political process has dismissed God's plan for decision making and adopted a more secure guarantee for peace called *Robert's Rules of Order*. In this traditional leadership role, the pastor is placed in a very difficult position as he is asked to moderate the meeting in hopes of maintaining order between opposing personalities. This process often causes problems between the pastor and his congregation. However, some pastors are afraid of losing control of the meeting and therefore would not want to hand off this role to another. Many believe we need this procedure to conduct the business of the church. Yet, the Bible makes no distinction between business versus spiritual decision making.

I have been in many meetings where the use of secular means to arbitrate order only ended in chaos and disunity. Besides, if a 51/49 majority rule occurs, the congregation is still divided. We are not a civic club. We are the body of Christ. Biblically speaking, division is simply not an option. I imagine that you can identify with what I am saying. Even so, the very issue of church authority is rigged for division not matter how we sugar coat it.

Decisions will always need to be made. Why can't the leaders and the congregation pray through the issues at hand until the Head reveals which decisions should be made? God's answers would always be best and more incredible than anything our common consensus could propose (Isaiah 55:9). Traditional democracy makes it too easy to ask for a show of hands. However, it takes time and waiting to hear from God which is why we usually do not. In short, our traditions have taught us to make decisions without God—how tragic. This is precisely why the church's vision is rarely larger than its self-absorbed organization. Additionally, God's supernatural leadership and provision are no longer needed to accomplish our shortsighted man-made goals. Consequently, we are consumed with maintaining our organizational structure and sustaining the traditions of men instead of fulfilling His global mission.

We have been tethered by the right foot to the wrong anchor. The trees of traditionalism are well rooted and have held the church in check for centuries. Why? Because it's been this way for generations. Consequently, the church has forgotten what it was like to be free. As a result, we are easily chained by another hindrance called legalism.

Chapter Three

Tethered to Legalism

Many elephants like to repeatedly try to break their chains in an attempt to get free.

Legalism and grace are sometimes seen as two opposing forces when it comes to matters of Scripture. It is the intention of this writer to clarify God expects His children to follow His directives completely while at the same time fully living in the grace He has provided. Therefore, when using the term "Legalism" we are talking about a rigid set of rules (both spoken and unspoken expectations) that tether followers of Christ to the institutional church. Legalism corrals God's people and hinders them from enjoying their freedom to follow the Holy Spirit's leading in a multiplicity of ways (i.e. giving, ministry, worship, testimony, service, etc.).

However, the structure itself is not the culprit here. The local church needs structure, but not to the extent it robs people of their freedom in Christ. Legalistic churches are very controlling and manipulate people through obligatory statements (i.e. being faithful to the local church or growing to be a good Christian). Teaching believers that serving exclusively in a particular local church is synonymous with serving Christ is the sentiment that eventuates in predictable bondage and fruitlessness. In other words, many legalistic churches psychologically cement their members to their local vision, making little allowances for them to be involved where God is moving outside their local church. Legalistic churches frown upon their members getting involved with other church ministries—especially if it is across denominational lines.

"Good Christians"

Many legalistic churches spend much of their time training their membership how to be good Christians. But, what does the phrase "good Christian" mean? Generally, church-goers believe this phrase depicts one who should live morally, attend church services, give money, witness, as well as read the Bible and pray. However, when believers are questioned how well they are doing in these areas, many will respond, "Well, I don't read my Bible or witness, etc. as much as I *should...*" The church has propagated a system of works that "please the Lord" and thousands are shackled by guilt because their works do not often fit this criteria. Consequently, they really do not enjoy their relationship with God but feel inadequate to please Him. Although most of us would say salvation is not *received* through works of man, we need to include neither is salvation *kept* by the works of man (Romans 10:9-10; Ephesians 2:8-9).

Those of us caught in the web of legalism subconsciously feel if we have spent time reading our Bibles or praying, we are somehow worthy to enter God's presence. However, if we have been extremely busy and have not read our Bibles or had our quiet time, then we cower before God like a dog with its tail tucked between his legs. We feel unworthy to approach God as if He were mad at us for not reading and praying. As a result, when sin enters our lives we are racked with guilt and shame. Those in bondage to legalism have a hard time forgiving themselves for falling into sin or worse yet, running headlong into it. This legalistic approach to God is exactly the opposite of His desire for us (Ephesians 3:11-12; Hebrews 4:16).

Congregations meet from week to week with an unspoken legalistic standard. Those who are saved come to church on Sunday mornings. While those more serious about God and His church attend on Sunday evenings. Further, those who are committed attend church on Wednesday evenings. But those who are really consecrated attend visitation nights, hold leadership positions, serve on committees, and attend every service. This modern day Pharisaism serves only to heap guilt upon the body of Christ thus, imprisoning them all the more to legalism.

Sadly, many ministers have developed this same attitude and use the pulpit to regularly harp on church attendance and commitment. Consequently, guilt becomes an obligatory motivator for people to attend church or participate in any Christian activity. After awhile, a steady dose of legalistic expectation trains the congregation to hold others accountable for mere attendance leaving one to think if a service is missed, the greatest apostasy imaginable has been committed. Yet, there seems to be very little expectation for following hard after Christ. We have been taught "to serve the institution is to serve God." Tragically, our Christianity is wedged between church activities, career, family, and recreation. The average believer trying to be a good Christian spends most of his time running to services, meetings, choir practices, seminars, retreats, and the like, and very little time actually serving Christ.

Furthermore, when we talk about faithfulness to the church our indisputable conceptual belief is the building with four walls. Faithful church attendance is underlined with the vehement conviction that we are not to "forsake the assembly" of believers. But what if the church lives outside the walls of our institutional thinking? What if we can "go to church" all week long and all day long? What if the church really is "out there—instead of in here?" Why do we feel almost entirely shackled to the services offered by our existing establishment when it comes to going to church? I'll tell you why—legalism.

If one readily admits he has not attended a church service from week to week, well-meaning believers verbally badger this person as if he had committed a great sin. The fact this person may have been involved in being the church all week long has little credence in the eyes of the legalist if services are not regularly attended. The legalist strongly believes that going to church is the optimum standard measuring faithfulness.

Is it possible to gather with believers all day every day? If we pray at work or play or worship together outside the institutional structure, are we not participating in the assembly of believers? Do we have to be present in "The House of God" to experience genuine fellowship with other believers? Our paradigm of church is saturated with centuries of legalistic thinking. And for some, to view the church outside traditional thinking is absolute heresy. How insidiously demonic—Satan has shackled us inside our legalistic walls, all the while mocking us for not permeating our culture.

I am not saying church attendance is not a good thing. But the probing questions in my mind are, "If this is so good for us, then why are so many marriages falling apart among faithful church-goers? Why do so many teens who grow up in church get to college and slip into the free-fall of sinful temptations? Why is the so-called body of Christ filled with impurities of every kind rendering her spiritually impotent? How can we profess to worship the God who created the universe and be so powerless to impact our eroding culture?" I'll tell you why, because our Shepherds have forgotten their number one job is to equip the saints. Instead, they spend a great deal of time securing their own survival with slick presentation and indoctrinating dogma that endears people to their church. Legalism has eclipsed the vision of our leaders. Instead of teaching others how to know Him, we are teaching the body of Christ how to be holy, pure, and faithful along with an entire list of sermonic directives aimed at creative disciplines to earn the favor of God. Make no mistake—preachers and other leaders may not call it legalism. But that is exactly what it is. The proof is in the fruit we produce, or the lack of it.

The problem is pastors have forgotten their job is to preach *messages* and not mere *sermons*. Messages can take the form of didactic instruction as well as prophetic directives. Messages come from God and sermons come from men. Sermons can often be the words of others. Messages are the words of One. The only men who get messages from God are those who spend vast amounts of time with Him. These men are God's men—God's messengers. They often weep when they deliver God's Word to His church. In short, they are not hard to recognize. Why does the church tolerate such slouchy declarations of God's eternal truths? Sadly, legalism has spawned a lot of preachers but very few true men of God.

Congregationally speaking, legalism keeps us busy to the extent that we no longer have time to breathe. Add to this schedule the normal busyness of rearing a family, and there is very little time to disciple others or reach a lost world. Consequently, we constantly feel as if God is not getting our personal best all the while very busy with church related activities. Legalism and the expectations imposed by the church deny intimacy with our Lord amidst the hectic pace of life.

This merry-go-round of life causes us to forget we cannot do anything to make Jesus love us *more* and neither can we do anything to make Him love us *less*. We need to remember in His presence there is fullness of joy (Psalm 16:11). We need to be reminded there are no elitist in God's army and we all share in the victory of our Commander in Chief. The rewards we receive will be given in direct proportion to how much we loved and served God not how much we attended services or read our Bibles. In order to be set free from legalism, we must accept God's unfathomable love. Our performance as a good Christian has no bearing on our eternal reward. We cannot accomplish anything for Him without Him. In truth, the rewards we receive actually belong to Him. Because of His grace, He allows us to share in those rewards for eternity. What a loving God we serve. There is no room for educational, financial, or spiritual self-aggrandizement in God's economy of faithfulness.

If it is true that we can do nothing to make God love us any more than He already does—And if it is true that we can no nothing to make Him love us any less, then why do we struggle to find value before God? Holiness, righteousness, and purity are all works of His Spirit within us. They come to fruition as we walk with Him. Therefore, our legalistic attempts at living with these characteristics are ludicrous at best. Only God can bring about these traits within His children. As we learn to walk daily in His presence, He is the one who develops and conforms us to His character.

New Experiences?

One good aspect of legalism is that it has created a deep desire in much of the believing community for more of God. Discerning believers realize there is much lacking in today's church when it comes to spiritual depth. Therefore, they are always yearning for that fresh work or movement of God. Although this may sound wonderful and greatly spiritual, it has deep pitfalls if not closely examined through the lens of Scripture.

As stated earlier, without the center hub of discipleship, many hungry believers have nowhere to attach their spokes of belief. As a result, they are very unstable in all their ways as they attempt to navigate the spiritual terrain around them. Consequently, as their desire for a fresh movement of God supersedes their spiritual maturity, they often fall prey to Satan's schemes of sensationalism. In an effort to escape the shackles of the churches rigorous legalism, many run headlong to every form of godliness or charismatic leader to whom they come in contact. Their motto seems to be, "just give me anything that appears to have life and I will embrace it!" Note the following examples.

Years ago, when the supposed "Toronto Blessing" was occurring, I traveled to Europe on a disciple making mission. During our free time, we decided to visit the catacombs of the Russian Orthodox Church. As we journeyed by candlelight deeper into the tunnels, our guide made the comment that many of the pilgrims searching for further inspiration travel deeply into these catacombs and can often be heard "barking like dogs or roaring like lions." Interesting. Barking like dogs and roaring like lions were the same characteristics attributed by many in Toronto as evidence of a great movement of the Holy Spirit in one's life. There we were in a literal tomb surrounding by dead bodies. Death was all around us where these same noises were manifesting themselves. Could these truly be the work of the Holy Spirit—barking and roaring? Hardly. I'm not being sarcastic. I just can't picture anyone in the first century church crawling around on all fours barking and roaring and praising Jesus all in the name of worship.

Then there are those who simply water down the offense of the cross by declaring how much God loves us as exemplified through the sound of raindrops or the sound of the wind. There concepts of "inspiration" are altogether earthy in tone and depleted of any semblance of judgment or sin. Others say we need to gather and soak up His presence and whatever comes to mind first is God's

Word. Still others would have us sit in a circle around someone who clears their mind and suddenly receives God's indisputable Word for each individual making up the circle.

There are a myriad of visualization techniques out there. These are all modern day emergent methodologies or derivatives thereof for fresh new ways of experiencing God. My question is, "Why are we so afraid to be held accountable?" When one individual carries too much power, look out! Deception is not far behind. Every heresy known to man begins this way. The deadness of legalism has encouraged young leaders to forsake many of the biblical directives in pursuit of new revelations from God. These revelations promise to bring a fresh new outpouring of God's presence as He is discovered through new forms, methodologies, and experiences. But new forms of worship or revelations will never increase *substance*. And therein lies the problem. The church of our day has totally lost concept of the substance of Christ alone! We cease to uphold Him, recognize Him, and genuinely worship Him. Consequently, many are looking for Him elsewhere.

Can anyone see the dangers here? For many today, their search for deeper intimacy with God has become a quest for some kind of supernatural phenomenon—a kind of celestial experience. Extremism seems to be the order for the day. While legalism produces dead orthodoxy without spiritual power, too much subjective experience leaves one completely vulnerable to all kinds of spiritual power. Problem? This power, is not from God. Just because something supernatural takes place does not mean it is from the Lord. If we simply rely upon subjective experience to validate truth, then each man can do what is right in his own eyes and completely justify his stance through experiential data. Experience in itself is not a valid test for spiritual truth.

However, there is a difference between experiences that can be validated by Scripture and those that cannot. Another negative about legalism is that it sometimes presets ones beliefs through indoctrination and therefore renders one inflexible in terms of accepting experiences outside their own. Individuals ensnared to legalism often display an attitude reflected in the following manner. If they have not experienced something (that is often clearly authenticated in the Word of God) then they dismiss it as unbiblical or explain it away by stating, "God no longer moves that way." And while I have already stated that experience in itself is not a valid test for truth, in this context—the lack of experience is not a valid test for truth either! If something supernatural can be seen in the Word of God, then it is authentic whether we have experienced it or not.

And so just as it is wrong to validate one's spiritual walk through experience alone, it can also be just as wrong to invalidate another's experiences due to your lack of those same experiences. Bottom line—we must have a plumb line by which to measure our experiences as to whether or not they are authentically from God. His written Word is that plumb line. Any experience that is not clearly revealed within the Scriptures themselves should be looked upon with great suspicion. Otherwise, each person's subjective experience becomes the catalyst to determine what is acceptable and what is not. You may trust your flesh to that extent, but I do not trust mine.

Furthermore, it needs to be stated here there are no new experiences that have not been experienced long before we were born. The modern expressions of these varied experiences can be traced back to all kinds of ecstatic phenomenon of the past. Much of what is being propagated today as "fresh" are old demonic forms of expression that were clearly opposed by the first century leaders as the mystical experiences of eastern cults, witchcraft, and sorcery were synchronized into Christian worship. The same kinds of people existed in the first century as do today— those who didn't believe anything and those who would believe everything. Interestingly enough, both groups often professed to possess the power of God; yet, they still often lacked the practical fruit of the Spirit in their daily lives.

Many non-Christian religions experience the same supernatural phenomenon as proclaimed in some Christian circles today but these people are not proclaiming Christ at all. Much is happening today through the deceptive vises of the evil one and undiscerning Christians are falling prey to it without thought or reflection. Some caught up in this practice may perceive deception is looming, but if they happen to renounce a certain experience the group is holistically accepting as "from the Lord," they are quickly ostracized as non-believing. This corporate legalistic attitude should be seen suspiciously all the more by the one who has been truly enlightened to the dangers before him. The discerning question needs to be, "Who receives the glory through this experience? Does man get the glory or does God?"

I can say with absolute certainty that pride always enters the arena when man is being exalted over God. Lips may render service and profess "glory to God" but aura and spirit tell the tale. If members of a group are sitting in awe of their leader and are afraid to challenge/question them, then the stage is ripe for deception. Keep your eyes and heart open to God's discerning Spirit and listen only to Him. Many who exalt themselves upon the platform of spiritual greatness will not be the ones God honors in heaven. Humility is the true mark of a genuine servant of God, not aura or reputation.

Sometimes I wonder if the people receiving the greatest eternal rewards will be those from non-western countries who serve God twenty-four hours a day and seven days a week without salary, benefits, or retirement. They have learned to fellowship with Christ through His sufferings. And that is enough for them. They are not casting aside what they deem as the old gospel in favor of the new for they have discovered that which is old (the crucified life) is what actually brings the new. Few of them are pastors of mega-churches with plaudits or degrees. Few of them are well known or have published a book. But they have what we in the Western church do not. They have a heart fully given to God. And this is what gets God's attention (2 Chronicles 16:9). When a believer enters the arena of willful submission, he pursues God for the sake of personal intimacy. The result is a much deeper, authentic relationship that necessitates personal worship more than that generated from obligatory habits or ecstatic experiences.

Someday, the legalistic church is going to wake up and set people free to serve Jesus with their time and money. This indescribable freedom through God's grace will sever our tethered legalistic faith and free God's people to wildly pursue Him with the totality of their being. We have tried breaking the chains long enough through works of our own and experiences of every brand. God has already broken the bond of legalism through Christ. But we must follow Christ His way. So, get out of your legalistic box, stop searching for emotional experiences, and live out your faith with passion for God! He is the one for whom we are searching. Freedom from legalism will go a long way to setting would-be disciples free, but there is still another hindrance we must acknowledge by which we are tethered—materialism.

Chapter Four

Tethered to Materialism

The quality of the chains is determined largely by the cost.

I read a story relating to the persecuted Church in China. These small house churches were made up of dedicated believers who lived in abject poverty. Yet, when one stated God had called them to another province to plant churches or conduct evangelistic campaigns, the congregation would sell their personal property in order to purchase a train ticket—even if it meant increasing personal poverty. Stories like this abound from around the world. Why don't we see this kind of sacrificial giving in the western Church on a regular basis?

In the western Church, Materialism has skewed our understanding of giving toward the Lord's work. We have been taught to secure the survival of the church, *first*. Then, we may give to other organizations if we have money left over. Several years ago, I was pastoring a small church which was meeting in a storefront building. Some well-meaning believers noticed our "need" for a more permanent location and offered to match dollar for dollar (up to $50,000) toward the construction of a new facility. We had just returned from a mission to Africa where our brothers and sisters desperately needed a structure in which to meet. My spirit was disturbed as I thought of my family overseas with no place to get out of the rain. At least we had a place to meet albeit temporary.

The idea emerged to approach our would-be donors about contributing to the costs of building several structures overseas first, and then work on constructing our facility. After all, we could build ten buildings overseas for the same cost of our one building. What a great opportunity to edify the Body of Christ! My idea was met with an icy reception. The comment was made, "If it is not constructed in America, then we are not interested in helping." Needless to say, we never received the money. This is a clear example of how Materialism has trained us to think only of ourselves. The selfish qualities of Materialism have created a lot of confusion in the Church when it comes to financial responsibility before the Lord especially in concepts relating to tithing, debt, and meeting the needs within the Body of Christ.

Tithing

First of all, many churches shackle the congregation to a very one-sided understanding of giving. Tithing is the main offering emphasized. However, tithing is not any more prominent in the Old Testament than the other offerings mentioned. Yet, many believers do not see any modern relevance in terms of functionality for the other offerings mentioned alongside the tithing principle. Why? I believe the main reason many church leaders focus almost exclusively upon the tithe is simply for self-preservation. Let me say believers should support the work of ministry in their local church. However, since many have focused almost entirely upon the tithe, giving in general has lost its place as worship. As a result, many seem to give out of obligation instead of a joyful heart (2 Corinthians 9:7).

Giving through the offering of "First Fruits" provided the children of Israel an opportunity to give the first and most succulent fruit of their crops to the Lord (Exodus 23). This offering was given not knowing if another crop would be forthcoming. The next crop depended upon the weather and therefore, the offering was a complete surrendering in faith to a continual provision from the Lord. This feast was established to exercise the faith of God's children and to remind them He was in control of their future provision and that all they possessed belonged to Him. God's people were to offer Him their very best...freely, lovingly, and willingly. This was God's desire.

Then, there was the "Free Will" offering that one doesn't hear much about in today's Church. The free will offering gave the people of God the opportunity to give above and beyond what was required by the Law. Why don't churches make this allowance for individuals instead of responding jealously toward all outside giving? Because Materialism is possessive and competitive, it is not open-minded to supporting other ministries but is determined to keep most available resources for itself. If you disagree with this statement, I encourage you to investigate how much of your church's annual budget is invested outside the local body. If the majority of your church's annual budget is appropriated outside the local body, then, congratulations—the Church you attend is an exception.

The transformed believer is supposed to live a lifestyle of giving. The giving of ourselves and finances is to be a natural outgrowth of God's love within us. However, most believers are so heavily in financial debt this part of the Christian transformation eludes them. We have lost the ability to wait upon God's provision as credit cards, lines of credit, and banks offer immediate provision.

Debt

A second area of confusion manifests itself when the pulpit declares how God's people need to eliminate personal indebtedness and even offers study courses to do so. Yet, when it comes time to "expand the opportunity to reach people," these same leaders launch capital fundraising campaigns that ask people to pledge (go into personal debt again) for years. These pledges go toward paying the church's debt. After the conclusion of the first fundraising campaign, there is often a second campaign which lasts for an additional number of years. Wait a minute. If personal debt is not pleasing to God, then why is the corporate debt of the church permitted? When church leaders depict this type of fund raising in their efforts to construct new facilities, it confuses anyone who is still able to think for himself. As a result, efforts to expand the institutional machine gobble up much of the available disposable income for *local* visions and dreams and dissolves what could have been given spontaneously and cheerfully toward *global* impact.

This process allows Materialism to raise another beastly head—Extravagance. Many churches are quite flamboyant with their facilities and rarely question the value of the monies spent. This unquestioned affair with Materialism is perhaps even choking out our opportunity to reach the world. For instance, in a day of multi-million dollar facilities, has anyone figured how many people could be led to Christ with the dollar figure spent on maintenance alone?

We need to ask the hard questions. Can we accomplish just as much ministry with a less expensive structure both in maintenance and construction costs? If the money given during a capital fund raising campaign was there to be given all the while, why weren't the people giving it already? For every dollar spent on the facility, would the congregation be willing to match each dollar toward missions giving? Does God really want us to give away thousands of dollars toward interest payments? Is there a better way to raise money? Churches have tried banquets, prayer meetings, solemn assemblies, and the like, but the end result is still usually a visit to the bank. Why do we need such colossal facilities in which to meet only a few times per week? I have often wondered how many architectural designs were simply to feed egos.

It is often embarrassing for me to bring brothers and sisters from around the world into our gigantic plush buildings. Almost always, their mouths fall open in utter amazement. A few of them have even wept from the sheer sadness of it all. You see, they are acutely aware of what this kind of funding in their nation could do for the Kingdom. The heart of God must break when He sees countless thousands of His children passing into eternity without knowledge of Him while we belabor raising more funds for mere steel, concrete, and mortar.

Several years ago, I observed a fellow seminary student weeping as he had just returned from Argentina. He was weeping because the American church he had spoken to the previous week was spending over one million dollars in order to renovate their sanctuary. He made the statement, "If they only knew how many they could lead to Christ with this money, I wonder if they would do otherwise?" We can object if we want to, but the use of money proves where our priorities really are. Are we Kingdom-focused or church-focused. Sometimes these two are not the same. As Jesus put it, "Where your treasure is, there will your heart be also" (Matthew 6:21).

I have often wondered what the Lord would do if we simply waited upon Him to provide the funds instead of promoting/ encouraging personal debt to do so. The church has adopted the same basic techniques for raising funds as other secular organizations, although we are great at spiritualizing them. I wonder how many financial miracles He would perform on our behalf if *He* determined our need for another building instead of committee consensus.

Make no mistake, God will allow us to go into debt for many years, but is this His best plan? Admittedly, many so-called "miracles" occur in the financial lives of individuals throughout capital fundraising campaigns. But are these changes wrought in the lives of believers because God is blessing the campaign or because these believers have rediscovered the joy of self-less sacrificial giving? It seems the joy would be much sweeter if the same sacrifices were made in order to change lives instead of construct buildings.

Shockingly, many church leaders have convinced the congregation when a building is completed, people will flock to the new structure. This is simply not so. How many beautiful buildings are half-filled each Sunday? In contrast, on a recent visit to poverty stricken India, I watched tearfully as those coming for worship rushed the worship center for a seat only to become lodged between the door facings. They literally became wedged between the door jambs as they hurried inside to worship our Lord. When the room was filled (for the third time—seating six hundred), the building erupted with praise as those from all walks of life praised the One who had set them free. When the offering was received *everyone* gave something. And I wept. I wasn't weeping for them, but for all of us in America who have forgotten the Holiness and awesome presence of the God we serve.

Perhaps, these followers of Christ didn't know when the building reached "eighty percent occupancy," no one else would come. Maybe they hadn't read the books by the western church growth gurus and were not aware of the barriers to Church growth. Maybe they were not concerned with church growth but simply reaching people with the Good News. By the way, within the last twenty years, this little church led to Christ and discipled over two hundred thousand people! Most of these converts who became disciples came from Hindu backgrounds and were extremely poor. Although stricken with poverty, Materialism had not wormed its way into their affections. India is not America and cultures are different. But the western Church is greatly preoccupied with gaining more members instead of discipling and sending out those we already have.

Needs of the Body of Christ/Community

Giving should be the natural outflow from every believer's life. Believers should give toward meeting the benevolent needs within the community without having to hold special offerings. We should give to our brothers and sisters in need within the Body of Christ without shame and embarrassment from either party. We should aid the orphan and the widow. Although many widows are very well taken care of here in the West, this is not the case in most underdeveloped countries. Why couldn't the church begin a ministry by widows to widows or children to orphans? We should freely give as the Spirit directs us to anyone anywhere. However, it seems our giving has become so mechanical and programmed we have lost the real joy of this privilege.

Sadly, many Church leaders preach all giving must come through the local church. And these leaders are afraid of what? Are they afraid if each member gives as the Lord directs there will not be enough money to run the institution? When people are taught to give to the Lord liberally as He directs, there will be enough to keep the institution running (including salaries). Maintenance and Materialism have clearly immobilized a great percentage of monies that could be leading a lost world to Christ. The money to reach the world is indisputably in the western church. We are simply spending it upon ourselves both personally and corporately all in an effort to gain more people. A good pastor friend of mine summed up our need when he stated, "I decided to stop praying for people to come to our church and started praying for God to show up."

Like the chains that tether the elephants, we have too long associated the costs of our buildings with value. The real value of the Church is her substance. Without substance, our buildings are nothing but mere shells. Have you ever noticed when God's presence fills the room time doesn't matter, padded seats do not matter, or nice clothing doesn't matter? Materialism has replaced our desire for the real presence of God and possessing so much we still find ourselves empty. Yet, Materialism is not the only cause for this void. In the modern Church, another chain has tethered us *outside* the throne room of God while our heavenly Father bids us to come *inside*. Individualism has chained us within—to that great enemy of God…Self.

Chapter Five

Tethered to Individualism

As for the quality of training of mahouts (trainers), here are disturbing signs that contemporary mahouts are losing many of the skills of the old days. This lack of skills is very likely in the near future to show up as poorer control of bull elephants, most of which are dangerous at least part of the time.

There are two inherent dangers looming on the horizon for the Church of our day. First of all, many leaders have lost their understanding of what it means to lead as God's appointed leader. Consequently, the Joshua's and Paul's of our day are few and far between. Secondly, amidst the confusion caused by the obvious missing components of the five-fold ministry, "The Church" is largely running out of control without accountability or biblical restraint. The need for disciple making among all believers has never been more needed than it is now. This is the only way to recover, rediscover, and harness the power and strength of the Body of Christ. And it is the *only* way to shatter the bonds of Individualism.

Seeking Personal Identity

Individualism is depicted in two forms in the modern Church. First, many pastors and or church leaders try to establish their *personal identity* through the church in which they serve. These leaders perceive other's view of the church as a direct reflection upon their leadership. Consequently, the size of the congregation, location of the facility, architectural design, salary figure, and community or denominational status, all play a major role in building self-esteem for some ministers. Are we truly seeking God's glory or man's?

For God has said, "I will not share my glory with another" (Isaiah 42:8). A leader's unconscious desire to "find himself" through the church's reputation dangerously leads to self-exaltation. Accordingly, this quest for individual personal identity has not only caused a lack of submission to one another but also to God. Consequently, we have set up ourselves for all kinds of failures when it comes to the ways of the flesh. How could God's appointed shepherds have forsaken faith and replaced it with self-exalting pride? The Scripture gives us a strong clue.

> "For the shepherds have become stupid, for they have not sought the Lord, therefore they have not prospered and all their flock is scattered" (Jeremiah 10:21).

When there is a problem in the Body of Christ, God comes looking for the Shepherd. The reason the flock is disunified and scattered today is because the Shepherds have become unresponsive to God. This word "stupid" means "dull of hearing."

Someone once said, "Rare is the man who can stand in the spotlight week after week without eventually being seduced by it."

Gradually, the spotlight and corporate position seduce many who become too busy to hear from God. In other words, church leaders no longer take time to hear God's voice and consequently end up ministering and preaching in the flesh. This lack of genuine searching for God has allowed Individualism to replace God's Glory. As a result, these leaders become driven by pride and self-ambition and thus evaluate their ministry with these questions. "Are my people growing? How big is my church? Will I be awarded by the denomination this year for recording the most baptisms?" These unspoken attitudes are very dangerous for the family of God. Just as Jeremiah stated, pride falsely exalts leaders who are stupid or dull of hearing.

In reality, for many leaders, pride becomes the primary driving motivator although it is rarely outwardly admitted but nursed deep within. In fact, without very carefully allowing the Holy Spirit to probe one's motives, these prideful attitudes can exist largely unnoticed by the average church leader. "Building the church" according to "my vision, goals and dreams" has led many away from the cross of Christ. Surprisingly to many, God never called His messengers to build the Church—that was to be His job (Matthew 16:18). God's leaders are to build *people*—not a numbers game preoccupied with growing the institution.

How did Christ's vision for the leadership and expansion of His Kingdom ever get so convoluted? During the first century, the Church met in groups of twelve to fifteen simply because this was all the average house could accommodate. Yet, they still managed to turn the world upside down. They did this without great numbers, education, or money. They possessed what we do not— substance. Faith in the power of God and faith in God Himself is what propelled them into the world (Hebrews 11:1). Leaders had faith in God not in themselves. Exalting individual personalities was not the focus but colossal corporate impact.

The modern Church has exalted the sermon to be the central purpose during congregational gatherings therefore making it easy for the pastor to be spotlighted as well. Even our architecture declares this malady—the pulpit sets upon an exalted platform in the center of the stage. It is indisputably the most prominent piece of furniture in the room. Many leaders parade themselves into the building as the service begins as if everything depended upon their presence. Can you imagine the early church operating in this fashion?

It appears the Scriptural purpose for the congregational gathering is not for the sermon alone, but congregational worship and spiritual intimacy both with God and one another. Clearly, it should not be the personality of the pastor or style of preaching/teaching that makes the event. To further expose the modern congregational preoccupation with preaching, it appears that most of the New Testament preaching was done among non-believers outside the walls of the congregational gathering place. Of course, there were discourses within the Synagogue or Temple. However, most of these occurrences had to do with defending the Gospel message against the backdrop of Judaism. Conduct a study for yourself and observe how much actual preaching is done among believers. Even so, I have known more than one pastor who became aggravated because the song service was too long and infringed upon his preaching time.

Whatever gave us the idea the sermon was the most important focus of the Sunday morning event? Is it our traditions, institutionalism, or education that teaches us this? Unfortunately, many of us who are called to proclaim the Word of God have bought into this line of thinking and as a result have exposed ourselves to many a pain. Man's ego is such a fragile emotional essence. It can be easily controlled by a simple yes or no. If preachers are not very careful with all the praise received, we begin to actually believe what we are hearing. Our prideful ego tells us, I am a great expositor—My sermons are anointed. Yet, many preachers expect this anointing to suddenly occur on Saturday evening as they prepare their message.

I heard a young pastor in seminary ask a question in preaching class as we were learning to prepare a sermon. He asked, "What I want to know is—what's wrong with getting on your face before the Lord until He gives you something to say?" I have never been able to get away from that question. Jesus summarized our acts of service when he said, "Apart from me, you can do nothing" (John 15:5). Individualistic pride often dilutes what could have been God's message into a mere sermon.

My lingering point is this: The message is a very important aspect of the Christian assembly, but there are other components of worship that are equally as important and sometimes more so. Preaching in the modern church has replaced teaching and training. Therefore, the average church is filled with those who warm a seat but respond with an icy reception to the real things of God. Preaching alone or an overemphasis upon preaching makes it too easy for the congregation to remain passively aloof. Unfortunately, preaching is the primary focus of many church leaders today.

Secondly, individual churches seek to establish their personal identity through the programs, ministries, or worship/teaching/preaching styles they offer. Many new churches are started each year as individuals look for the "missing element" in the Body of Christ. They don't seem to know exactly what it is, but they do know something is missing. Consequently, this hope gives birth to many new visions for church form and polity. The quest for a new corporate identity ensues. Even church leaders are searching feverishly for this missing element in the church. The illustrations throughout the rest of this chapter depict the church's quest to find this missing element.

Seeking Corporate Identity

Some have believed variations in *musical style* to be the missing element and consequently ushered in the period unofficially known as the "worship wars," that is, modern praise and worship choruses versus the historic melodies of hymnody. While not wanting to fall behind progress or lose members, many traditional churches have elected to blend the two forms of worship. Yet, other churches have done away with organs and pianos and replaced them with synthesizers and band instruments of every kind. Choirs have been replaced by worship teams and song leaders by ministers of music. Soloists are no longer introduced but quietly make their way toward the platform without fanfare. Often Scripture choruses are sung repeatedly with much emotional fervor, and yet, the basic format in order of worship changes very little because choruses have simply filled the slot where the hymns used to be.

Other leaders have stated the lack of *biblical church government* to be the major missing element. Therefore, the new church has been organized around a plurality of leadership called Elders. These Elders are quite often elected by the congregation or appointed by the pastor to make all the administrative decisions for the church while informing the people of the church's vision. Congregational polity has been replaced by the decision-making powers of the Elders. The pastor usually serves as a co-elder.

Still other leaders have believed the missing element to be *outreach*. As a result, the entire format of the church has been designed to reach unchurched Mary and Joe. Casual dress is welcomed and encouraged. Sermon topics reflect a basic moral lesson to reveal one's need for Christ or a more user-friendly approach to dealing with life's issues. Dramatic skits are often the center focal point of the service and usually follow the same theme as the sermon. Public invitations are shunned to keep from embarrassing interested seekers who are encouraged to talk with personal counselors concerning questions. Special events are planned to reach the local community and may include such enticements as hotdogs, cotton candy, music, and inflatables.

Still other churches have believed the missing element to be *missions* and therefore are constantly planning and sending missionaries both nationally and abroad. Backyard Bible Clubs, Vacation Bible School, construction teams, and evangelistic emphases are the norm. However, with all the going and sending, discipleship that leads to multiplication is rarely the objective.

Individualism may even take on corporate form as many of these new strategies involve moving to *new locations* of ministry. Some pastors believe they have discovered the missing element and have divided their former congregations in hopes for a new start. Thus, all involved have hopes of doing church the right way. Some churches combine some or all of the strategies aforementioned in hopes of discovering the missing element. These leaders often attend seminars or visit other churches to see how they are doing church. As a result, these leaders often mimic other's programs in hopes of reaping the same results.

Virtually every new church start has stories of God's miraculous provision for buildings or property. As God continues to lead in various ways, the mistaken assumption ensues—"We have entered into God's favor. God is blessing us because we are pleasing Him with our new strategy for doing church." A kind of unspoken self-righteousness evolves that reflects their individualistic attitude—"God is not honoring the work of other churches in the community or they would be growing like we are."

Often times, the newly planted congregation will also grow rapidly as those from other congregations join the pilgrimage to find the missing element. The unspoken statement often becomes the heartfelt sentiment—"The only place God is truly moving is in church." Slowly the unmistakable monster of pride inevitably grieves the Spirit of God. After the newness wears off (usually around two to five years) people begin losing their enthusiasm (vision) despite the best efforts of leaders to keep something exciting before them. Gradually, the newness becomes a rut. Despite new music, government, outreach, evangelism, or missions, the new church eventually reverts back to the same old system in function—the very same dilemma they had originally hoped to escape.

The congregation becomes ensnared by a new version of the old system—a telltale sign the new church start has institutionalized itself. Older believers complain of "not being fed by seeker sermons." Original visionaries get tired of carrying the administrative responsibilities (nursery care, parking, setting up and taking down temporary facilities, etc.). Consequently, many original founders or older members decide to search elsewhere for the missing element and the growing new church begins to decline. If growth continues, the church is constantly filled with new members with a revolving back door for those leaving the membership. This process ordinarily happens so quickly that it usually gives rise to a leadership crisis—too many members and not enough leaders.

The Church is then pressured to elect or appoint more leaders who have not been tested nor tried and consequently sentences itself to untold amounts of conflict. When conflicts begin, the original pastor often finds a new place for ministry or the new church loses another segment of its membership as they leave to start anew...again. Eventually, the promising new start that was supposed to reach a city simply becomes just another church. The new Individualistic identity dies as the quest for the missing element continues. America's cities, suburbs, and small towns are littered with churches fitting the above descriptions. And there is relational carnage lying everywhere to prove it.

These are disturbing signs for they are greatly hindering the fulfillment of the Great Commission. And we have much in common with both the mahouts and elephants described at the beginning of this chapter. Unless modern biblical trainers (leaders) rediscover the skill of the "old days" (biblical directives), the church will remain shackled and unpredictably dangerous. As long as the church is tethered with the chain of Individualism, the true power she possesses will never be realized. Will leadership remain restrained by the self-propagating strategies/ideas/methodologies of men, or will we erupt from the very throne room of God endowed by His power and strategy to reach the world? The answer remains to be seen.

Part 2

The Untethered Church

Chapter Six

Discovering the Missing Element

"For I know the plans that I have for you," declares the LORD, "plans for welfare and not for calamity to give you a future and a hope. Then you will call upon Me and come and pray to Me, and I will listen to you. You will seek Me and find Me when you search for Me with all your heart."

Jeremiah 29:11-13

If God is able to do all He is doing through a system that He did not orchestrate, imagine what the church could accomplish if God's full power was poured out upon His people. Unmitigated power, resolve, surrender, and worship would be the result. The world would have no problem recognizing the people of The Way. Yet, we remain chained to a man-made system—encumbered, weak, and ineffective in fulfilling Christ's mandate to make disciples of all nations. Something is missing.

What if the missing element we are searching for is the *very real presence of God*? With all of our attempts to fix the problems of the institutional church, we have forgotten one very important truth—God doesn't fully bless that which is not His. Is it possible that while we pretend His presence is among us, in reality His Spirit is grieved due to our disobedience and tolerance for sin? His Spirit will not be fully manifested in man-made organizations or strategies. Oh, that the Church in this century would live out her faith explosively so our dying world could see the life-changing power of God!

One of my friends has said, "The church today is akin to the farmer who stands at the barn door and beckons the crops to come in and join him." Have you ever wondered how the world reacts to church marquees such as the following examples?

> End of the season special, free salvation with baptism included.
>
> Come on in, we'll scare the hell out of you!
>
> You said you would visit us, now do it!
>
> Free trip to heaven, inquire inside.
>
> What is missing in our ch_ _ch? UR!
>
> We need NEW members!
>
> Jesus is coming soon! Don't miss the flight.
>
> Which seat will you have for eternity? Smoking or Non-Smoking?
>
> Ribbit, Ribbit. Where will you go when you croak?

Hey, when all else fails, just use the direct approach, right? Yes, these were taken from real church marquees—no wonder the world doesn't take us seriously. We are throwing slogans at the lost trying to coax them into joining our institution. It is all quite amusing to those who do not understand the Christian faith. They drive past our barred compounds completely insulted while we enjoy peanut fellowships all the while congratulating ourselves for our clever antics. These slogans are at best—corny, embarrassing, and greatly demeaning to the glory of Christ. Personally, I don't think many of us could stand beneath the scathing rebuke from our Lord if He were to have some say so in the matter. We have completely trivialized all that is holy to Him. Enough said.

We have forgotten the mission is to lead others to Jesus and disciple them in their faith. Every believer is to be a reproducer. Somewhere along the line, we substituted the real mandate for the people of God into merely inviting people to Church. It appears we have lost the ability to lead others to Christ before they enter the church doors. To borrow another adage from my great friend Herb Hodges, "the contemporary church's motto seems to be—come inside and go to heaven or stay away and go to hell." We have tried everything to get them to come to us and forgotten our command to go to them. As a result, our drawing ability is now equated with the same appeal as other religions—most of which do not represent the truths of Christ. Sadly, when we do manage to talk someone into visiting our church, they usually do not discover the missing element and politely refuse our next invitation.

To emphasize—the missing element in many churches today is the *presence of God.* We have tried almost every conceivable strategy to reach people and forgotten the simple words of Christ, "...for apart from me, you can do nothing" (John 15:5). If we lift Him up as both Savior (crucified) and Lord, He will draw men unto Himself (John 12:32). This is precisely why genuine worship is of major importance when we gather together as God's redeemed children. The church today must rediscover the presence of God in her midst. Quite simply, we must seek *Him.*

Chapter Seven

Embracing the Solutions

And no one pours new wine into old wineskins.
If he does, the wine will burst the skins, and both
the wine and the wineskins will be ruined. No, he
pours new wine into new wineskins.

Mark 2:22

Finally, let us examine some possible solutions to our tethered frustration. We must embrace what the Lord is doing in the life of His church. Below, I have listed several areas in which I perceive God to be working. The following examples are by no means exclusive.

Embracing House Churches

Suppose the church decided to adopt the Ephesians 4 model depicted throughout this book. What would this church look like? There is very little information on the specifics of New Testament church worship. We know believers met together in homes where they prayed, worshipped, shared and ate together (Acts 2:46-47) and often taught the Scriptures. However, there is very little information when it comes to form or format. This raises two interesting questions. The first question is—did God originally desire for churches to grow large numbers and stay together in one place? Or, did God intend for the church to multiply when she outgrew someone's home, thus, spreading the Church's ministry throughout multiple locations?

I once met a pastor in Burkino Faso, Africa, who served a church that had adopted the latter strategy. The church was running one thousand in worship but the pastor became convicted of his disobedience and led the people to start praying toward planting new churches instead of growing their congregation larger. Several hundred people sold their homes and moved to a new location where previously there had not been a Christian witness. The last time I checked, this church had planted over twenty churches using this same approach.

Westerners do not think this way. The average believer moves their family to a location based upon employment and then seeks a church they hope will meet their needs. Churches have catered to this expectation and now we have everything from babysitting services to parking attendants. We are consumed with trying to reach numbers while forgetting that quality is what matters in God's economy. The first century church appears to have been made up of thousands of house churches who stormed their world for Christ impacting both culture and the future. Without a doubt, their main focus was upon multiplication instead of addition.

Currently, the house church movement is planting thousands of small home-based cells. This very well may be God's answer to the western dilemma. Although much of the programs offered by large churches are not practical to offer in a small setting, believers meeting in house churches readily understand this. However, this fact alone discourages some believers from attending a small assembly that doesn't provide child care. The average believer is spoiled to getting their needs met. But the house church movement is not the answer in itself to finding the missing element. One of the dangers of the house church movement is that it is sustained by those who are tired of the traditional church format. If these new church cells are not very careful, they too will institutionalize and forget multiplication is the mandate. Additionally, they may possibly function without the five-fold ministry mentioned in Ephesians. As a result, they will run in the same circular pattern as the larger traditional churches only with less effort.

The Ephesians 4 model could easily operate within a small cell group network just like it did in the New Testament. Small groups are easier to manage and intimacy is easier to achieve among the brethren. Money can be given directly to ministry projects since funds are not exhausted supporting salaries and maintenance costs. Mission projects can be hands on for everyone instead of the elite few of larger congregations. Furthermore, accountability is easier to achieve in small groups than in large numbers.

It needs to be stated the first century church was not perfect but riddled with problems. However, the difference between them and us is they relied upon God appointed leaders and the Scriptures to bring rebuke, correction, and encouragement. This is accomplished much easier in a small group setting than in a larger context.

Embracing Balanced Leadership

Why do some have trouble believing God continues to manifest Himself through human vessels who willingly submit themselves for His purposes? It appears the Apostle, Prophet, Evangelist, Pastor, and Teacher were all to be mutually submitted to one another, although the Apostle was to be the leader of the leaders. If the proper biblical system of checks and balances is maintained, there is no room for self-aggrandizement or abuse of power. All remain submitted to the head of the church who is Christ. Instead of the Holy Spirit leading the church where God's appointed leaders lead with spiritual discernment and love for the body of Christ, our traditions and democratic ways have created an almost completely self-absorbed church. Consequently, there is no real connection or spiritual awareness as to what God is doing globally among the body of Christ.

Admittedly, many who have adopted this Ephesians 4 model for church leadership have entrusted too much power to the apostolic office. In many of these churches (mostly charismatic) the apostle carries a big stick and basically calls the shots. This model exemplifies the opposite extreme as the previous models discussed. What is needed is balance in leadership authority.

The Apostle Paul and others were simple men just like we are today. God allowed His chosen leaders to record the Scriptures which were delivered to men once and for all. This was one of the unique ways God used the biblical writers. However, the miraculous works recorded throughout the Bible were manifested through the power of the Holy Spirit. And we know that He is still alive today and desirous to work through His appointed leaders.

Embracing God's Power

The Holy Spirit's power is still active throughout the world. Whether His manifestations are a part of our denominational experience or not does not invalidate His power nor His manifestations. The fact is we need His presence now more than ever. Sadly, many churches have domesticated the Holy Spirit. They tell Him when and how they are comfortable with Him working. As long as He doesn't do anything extraordinary, they tolerate Him within the confinements of their protective doctrinal box. We can no longer act as if all is well. Our land is being engulfed by every strategy Satan can muster while we remain tethered inside our self-absorbed theological zoos. We need a movement of God's Spirit in tsunami proportions to wake us up! Yet, many believe His power in these dimensions has ceased or is rare. They believe the trumpeting herald of His presence and miraculous power were lost after the first century.

But why would God stop revealing Himself through miracles after the first century? Some would say it was because the Scriptures were given. Yet, the New Testament Church was sharing copies of the Scriptures, but they still experienced miracles. Are we saying after the Scriptures were collated the miraculous power of God was no longer needed to validate God's Word? If this is the case, then after the Scripture is translated into the language of those who have never heard the gospel, miracles should cease. Yet, we know from reports all over the world, this is not the case. Why then the apparent cessation of common place miracles in America? Could it be the people of God have been led *away* from God by the very ones who claim to be leading us *to* God? Could it be because we have embraced a system of men that is void of the sanctioning presence of God?

At the time of this writing, I have been traveling the world for almost fifteen years now, and I can't think of anything mentioned in the Bible I haven't at least heard of overseas. I am aware of entire villages coming to Christ after the lame walked or the blind opened their eyes. These indisputable miracles validate the power of God against the backdrop of heathenism and idolatry. No one can argue with the power of God's miraculous work and deliverance once these signs take place. This is exactly what was happening in the New Testament against the backdrop of extreme paganism.

God is still God and His power has not been diluted one iota. Could it be true that God will not move where there is unbelief or where organizational methods have replaced His Spirit? We have been doing the same thing for decades and have lost our plumb line for faith. As a result, the church has become weak and powerless as she depends upon her own leadership, programs, and strategies to grow the corporate giant. If the church is to break free from the tethering posts mentioned in this book, we must embrace the supernatural power of God in order to do so. God still wants to use His miraculous power to enable His People to knock down anything standing in their way when it comes to propagating the kingdom.

Embracing a Call to Arms with Boldness and Wisdom

There are many well-intentioned church leaders today who truly possess a heart for God and long to see His people become the New Testament church. However, there are also those who have been seduced by the worldly system that has invaded the body of Christ. They have become professional leaders. Yet, for the sake of their personal welfare, many are afraid to confront the system as it stands today. As a result, we continue to hand this upside-down system to each successive generation. Tragically, we are diluting the power of God to impact our society and are headed down the same pathway as Europe.

Many leaders today greatly desire to serve the Lord. However, like David trying to wear Saul's armor, we find ourselves greatly encumbered by the institutional and traditional expectations of men. If we are to follow the Lord and charge into battle, we must be free from that which binds us (Hebrews 12:1-3). We must cast ourselves at His feet and cry out to the One who has called us. We must confess our confusion and disobedience and rely completely upon Him to secure our financial welfare and provision. We must make a hard course correction if the impact upon our culture is to change.

However, the mountain these leaders must climb to incorporate this change is hazardous indeed. Nevertheless, this trek must take place if we are to regain God's favor. But this venture will be very costly to those in leadership and will require great courage and wisdom.

Those of us who are now actively leading traditional churches have the greatest decision to make. We can slowly institute change and gradually make the curve for the next generation of leaders, or we can immediately make a hard course correction. Know that to make a hard course correction at this point would surely be wrought with trials and emotional distress. The possibility of losing one's leadership role would be very probable. However, all new movements are paved with the carnage of those who instigated them. Nonetheless, it is much easier to read of someone else's courageous life than to sacrifice your own. It seems more prudent to begin a new ministry altogether in order to serve in the capacity God has called you, doesn't it? But even this venture will test your spiritual mettle. For reasons already covered in this book, newness is not always the answer. It's time to seek the Lord.

Leaders must hear the voice of the Lord and obey. It's that simple. Your task as a leader is to seek God's perspective as to how you fit into His plan for restoring His church. Then, clearly identify exactly what type of leader you are. Are you an appointed leader or elected leader? The exact direction God takes you after this is altogether up to Him.

I believe within the next few decades, we will see a great number of people (who have left traditional churches looking for the missing element) returning to more traditional orthodoxy. They will have discovered that informal song and dance was not what they were looking for and will continue searching for something with depth and purpose beyond informality. Yet, they will remain somewhat dissatisfied and possibly disillusioned deep within having not discovered the missing element. Could it be that our self-imprisoned and tethered predicament to Institutionalism, Traditionalism, Legalism, Materialism, and Individualism has permanently grieved The Holy Spirit? Could the churches lack of purity, holiness, power, and surrender be due to the fact that God's glory has departed—that His hand has been all but removed from the churches of our nation? It's time to bring back the glory.

Embracing a Fresh Passion to Follow God No Matter the Cost

There is good news. God is raising up a new generation of leaders who are not connected to denominational bureaucracy. Their motto is "Just Give Me Jesus." This generation is also looking for the missing element—only they are not afraid to cast off every restraint in order to find it. They are already aware the missing element is God's Presence and have been trying to express this to the older generations for some time.

The greatest hope for the church to break free of her tethered existence will be found in the quality of these new leaders. I believe these new leaders are now young adults, teens, and yet to be born. These new generational leaders will break free from the tethering posts and run wild in reckless abandonment to their King. Then, the church will experience the freedom and power for which she has been longing for centuries. But these new leaders must find a well-defined track waiting for them when they get to the starting line. Now is the time for the ground breakers to rise up, bow up, and plow hard!

This mandates current leaders begin handing off a more biblically accurate paradigm for leading the church when it comes to functionality and purpose. If the leaders now standing at the helm will show these new radical followers of Christ the course, they will surely set the sails according to His directions. And make no mistake about it, when other religions explore our tangled jungles of orthodoxy, the footprints of the church will unmistakably be clear—both in power and purpose! God will surely move among His children according to His perfect design and we will finally be free from the ecclesiastical chains that have bound us for so long.

But first, we must restore the spiritual knights who guard the treasure which has been entrusted to them (2 Timothy 1:14). These are God's appointed leaders of Ephesians chapter four. They are the keepers of the flame. At any cost, these leaders are to ensure that the fiery presence of God's Holy Spirit is never quenched nor grieved. They are the gatekeepers of the church with swords held high—those who guard against heresy, spiritual apathy, and deception. Their resolve is to make sure the missing element of God's presence is never missing again.

Epilogue

It is my opinion the prevailing traditional and institutional church sentiments mentioned in this book are beyond immediate repair. It's simply too high a hill for those spiritually out of shape to make the climb. Besides, if it's not broken, then why try to fix it? Surprisingly, many today (including leaders) see absolutely nothing wrong with the modern church. In their opinion everything is fine. They just need "to do better in a few areas."

Does this sound like the sentiment of spiritual warriors to you? Not to me, it doesn't. If this attitude continues, one day, after we rub the sand out of our eyes, we will look around and see Buddhist temples, Muslim mosques, and shrines of every dimension dotting the American landscape. The Muslim religion alone will overrun Christianity by their sheer numbers in the coming decades. Presently, their birthrate is approximately four times that of Americans. In fact, it is already taking place and the church chooses to stick her head back in the sand—business as usual. Although it may sound calloused, (just as it was in the days of Moses) I'm afraid a generation or two must pass away in order for the church to reclaim the land. In my opinion, if the tethered church doesn't change course rather quickly, she won't have to worry too much about the aforementioned religions, for she will self-destruct. Regardless of opinion, the church will either win our oppressors to Christ, or we will be overrun by them.

In spite of our tethered dilemma and glaring biblical incon-sistencies, God still does great things in our midst from time to time. Profound things are occurring in many churches. Perhaps, this is the greatest mystery of all. God, in His great mercy and love for us, moves through the church even when we sometimes miss His perfect will for us. How can God use ungodly leaders, politically-driven leadership, carnal church-goers, perverted motives, and institutional shallowness to accomplish His work? There is only one answer—because He is God. However, just because God sometimes uses us in our fleshly self-governing institutionalism, doesn't mean He doesn't desire more from us. This is no reason to remain in our present state. Questions need to be asked honestly and answers need to be faced squarely. The conditions I have stated and the conclusions I have drawn have come from my passion for God's presence in my life and ministry. May we all continue to grow in God's Word and work in His world. We need to arm ourselves with humility and truth.

May church leaders today fall before Christ's feet in reckless abandonment until a new vision arises ... a vision of the unshackled church full of grace and truth—a vision of the church in her fully intended freedom and power—a vision of the church that stampedes the jungles of darkness tearing down everything in her way ... And I can hear the screeching voices of Satan's demonic hordes as they scurry to get out of the way, "The church is finally free and not even our gates can prevail against her!" I think this is exactly what Jesus was talking about (Matthew 16:18). What do you say?

Also from Tim Miller

Jesus Trained Disciples to Multiply. You Can Too!

The goal of every disciple maker is to produce fully mature disciples of Christ who are able to develop more disciples.

This manual is useful in training disciples in the local church as well as abroad. The simple strategy and easy-to-follow format make this an ideal tool for small groups, discipling new believers, preparing for mission trips, and equipping leaders overseas to train disciples.

Creation points to the Creator.

Every sportsman has them. Stories—and lots of them. The stories in Seasons of Reflection come from Tim Miller's 40-plus years as an outdoorsman. Entertaining as they may be, the stories are not the point. Tim's love for God has been enhanced through these experiences. And *that* is the point.

Tim shares some of the life lessons he has learned while experiencing God in the great outdoors. Join Tim on the hunt for what really matters.

To order these resources, or additional copies of *Tethered* visit www.disciplethenations.com or call 270-839-0649.

About the Author

Dr. Tim E. Miller is President of DTN, an international disciple-making ministry. He has pastored seven churches and holds a Masters of Divinity and Doctoral degree in Ministry. He has ministered in many foreign nations throughout Africa, Asia, and Europe. He often serves as the keynote speaker for discipleship meetings, retreats, and conferences.

For more information visit www.disciplethenations.com or call 270-839-0649.